Nathan Levy's

STORIES WITH HOLES VOLUME 22

By Nathan Levy

A collection of original thinking activities for improving inquiry!

A Nathan Levy Books, LLC Publication

Copyright © 2020 Nathan Levy Books LLC

All rights reserved. No part of this book may be reproduced in any manner whatever, including information storage or retrieval, in whole or in part (except for brief quotations in critical articles or reviews), without written permission from the publisher. For more information, contact us at:

Nathan Levy Books, LLC
18 Moorland Boulevard
Monroe Township, NJ 08831
Nlevy103@comcast.net
Phone- 732-605-1643
Fax-732-656-7822

ISBN – 978-0-9997908-8-5

Copyright © 2020 Nathan Levy Books, LLC

Cover Art by Dallin Orr – www.dallinorr.com

Printed in the United States of America

PREFACE – by Nathan Levy

This book is the result of several years' accumulation of ideas leading to puzzling stories that lend themselves to what I call thinking games. The "games" have become the means for thousands of people to carry on a totally enjoyable process of engaging critical and imaginative thinking. Volume 1 of my Stories with Holes is a collection of stories that has been gathered from various sources. Nathan Levy's Stories with Holes Volumes 2-22 are original. Wherever I speak I share some of the stories with my training groups. Teachers, parents and children enjoy the stories immensely. I hope you will as well.

INTRODUCTION

The objectives of using Nathan Levy's Stories with Holes include the following:

- to provide for growth in imagination and intuitive functioning
- to give experiences that display the fun of working cooperatively, rather than competitively, on a common problem
- to increase cognitive skills of resolving discrepancies through successful experiences
- to provide enjoyable changes-of-pace for task-oriented learning environments

This is a structured activity. It is designed to ensure involvement on the part of each participant, and to promote feelings of group and individual success.

The games are designed to accommodate all levels. "Children" from ages 8-88 will benefit from using these stories.

The time a story takes will vary. Usually a story lasts from 3 to 30 minutes, but some stories can take days. Children, lower grades through high school, tend to regard these thinking games as play instead of work. It is one of the few activities I know of that "hooks" almost anyone into creative use of their intelligence, i.e. learning, almost in spite of themselves. Nathan Levy's Stories with Holes are for all groups over age seven, regardless of background or achievement level.

**Please note that I have revised the above introduction and the following methodology from the way they appeared in the original collection of Stories with Holes. The revisions are based on my current workshop experiences with children and adults.

N.L.

METHODOLOGY

The first time a group plays, it will be necessary to begin by announcing something like the following: "I am going to tell you a story with a hole in it – I mean that an important part of the story is missing. Listen carefully so you can find the missing part, for the story may not seem to make much sense to you at first…"

At this point, tell the story once, pause, and then tell it the same way again. Then say…

"You can ask questions that can be answered either with a "yes" or with a "no". I can only answer "yes", "no", "does not compute", or "is not relevant". If I answer, "does not compute", that means that the question you asked cannot receive a straight "yes" or "no" without throwing you off the track."

Allow for questions about the process, if there are any, but usually it is best simply to jump into the game by having the questioning start. The process becomes clear as the game progresses. Once a group has played the game, the full directions given above for playing the game are unnecessary.

From this point on, answer only in one of the four designated ways. The following is an example of a computed story taken from <u>Stories with Holes</u>, and how it might be played:

Story: Mitch lives on the twentieth floor of an apartment building. Every time he leaves, he rides a self-service elevator from the twentieth floor to the street; but every time he returns, he rides the same self-service elevator only to the fifteenth floor, where he leaves the elevator and walks up the remaining five flights of stairs. Repeat, then ask who knows the answer already; if any do, ask them to observe and not give away the answer.

Sample questions participants might ask:
Question: Does the elevator go all the way up?
Answer: Yes.
Q: Does he want the exercise?
A: No.
Q: Does it have something to do with the elevator not working right?
A: No.
Q: Does he have a girlfriend on the 15th floor who he stops to see?
A: No.
Q: Does he have something different about him?
A: Yes.
Q: Is he a robber?
A: No.
Q: Is he a real person?
A: Yes.
Q: A tall person?
A: No.
Q: Is his size important?
A: Yes.
Q: I know! He's too short to reach the button!
A: Right!

At this point, make certain that all the participants understand the answer and why it is the correct answer. In the example given above, the group found the answer quite soon. Instead of starting a new game -- particularly if this is the first time playing – spend some time processing the game with questions like:

* What did you have to do in order to play this game? (Listen, hear each answer, think, imagine, follow a line of reasoning, eliminate possibilities, etc.)

* Ask the person who finally solved the riddle, "Joanne, did you have help from others in finding the answer?" It nearly always comes out that the person relied on previous questions and answers. Use this to point out the interdependence of players, and reduce competition within the group to be the "winner".

* When do you see yourself having to use the kind of thinking you use in this game?

 Usually a group of youngsters will be eager to try a second game right away.

Some important points to remember:

1. Immediately following the telling of each story and before the questioning begins, ask if anyone in the group has heard it before and knows the answer. Tell these people to observe and refrain from questioning.

2. Use the "does not compute" response whenever a single word or phrase in a question makes it impossible to answer with a "yes" or "no" answer. Examples from the story above:

- "Why does he live on the twentieth floor?" "Why" questions, as well as "where, who, when or which", cannot be answered "yes" or "no".

- "Does the elevator operator make him get off at the fifteenth floor?" No mention was made of an operator.

3. If a game goes past 10 or 12 minutes and some people begin to lose interest, close the game for the present. There is absolutely nothing harmful in leaving the puzzle unsolved. The group can return to it another time, when interest and energy are high. Some students may protest, but do not give the answer. The experience of non-closure provides some valuable learning in itself; but more importantly, once a group has expended considerable energy on the game, the victory should be an earned one. Although there may be some unusual circumstances under which you would give the group the answer, I have found it best not to do so (even if some are begging). The point here is not to "take the answer away by giving it." You can always return to it later. What is important is that the students earn the feeling of "we-did-it!"

4. Share the leader role. Once kids have learned how the game works, have a volunteer lead the game. He or

she must choose from the stories he or she already knows. As soon as you are convinced the student is familiar with the story, the answer, and the process (which you should previously have modeled) have the leader read the story to the class and begin taking questions. Most important here is what you model. A child-led game is an excellent small-group activity to have going on while you are occupied elsewhere in the classroom.

5. You may periodically want to encourage categorical thinking. When a player asks a question beginning, "Would it help us to know…" or "Does it have anything to do with…" pause in the game and show how the type of question is uniquely helpful in narrowing down the range of questions, distilling and focusing the group's attention, or cutting away large slices of the topic that are irrelevant. Thus, the question "Is David's occupation important?" tends to be more useful than "Is he a plumber? A teacher?" etc.

6. Be sure that a question is exactly true, or exactly false, before responding. One word can make the difference.

Unique Materials Published by Nathan Levy Books, LLC

A.C.T. 1: Affective Cognitive Thinking
Artistry
Beyond Schoolwork
Brain Whys
Breakfast for the Brain
Creativity Day-By-Day
Gifted Children and How Trauma Impacts Them
Nathan Levy's Intriguing Questions – Volumes 1-6
Nathan Levy's Stories with Holes – Volumes 1-22
Nathan Levy's Test Booklet for Every American
Perfectionism vs. the Pursuit of Excellence
Principles of Fearless Leadership
School Leaders' Guide to Trauma Sensitive Schools
Teachers' Guide to Resiliency Through the Arts
Teachers' Guide to Trauma
The Principals Recommend: 101 Great Activities for Student Learning and Brain Development
There Are Those
Thinking & Writing Activities for the Brain- Books 1 & 2
THINKology
Trauma Informed Teaching Strategies That Are Good For All
What To Do When Your Kid is Smarter Than You
Whose Clues? (Am. Hist., Mus., Lit., Sci., Sports, Authors)
Write from the Beginning

1. Taryn

Taryn had tuberculosis, angina, palsy, arteriosclerosis and eczema. She and her family were very happy. Why?

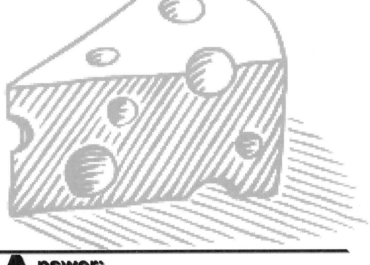

Answer:

They were words Taryn had studied for the spelling bee. She got them all correct during the contest.

2. Casper the Cat

Casper, our house cat, was outside during a snow storm. She had no collar, and it was at least an hour before we realized she was not in the house. Our search for our beloved cat was easy.

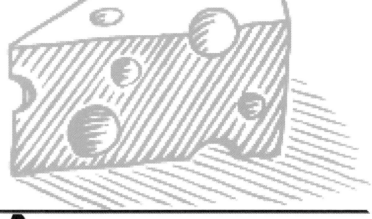

Answer:

Casper is a black cat. She stood out in the snow.

3. Jim the Wanted

Jim was wanted in three states. Even when surrounded by police in the three states he was wanted in, Jim was never arrested. He was behind bars in many instances without consequences. Why?

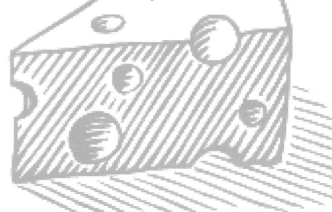

Answer:

Jim is water. The three states he is wanted in are liquid, solid and gas.

4. The Driver

HOV lane laws require two or more passengers per vehicle. When pulled over by a policeman, the driver and his friend were incensed that the policeman still gave the driver a ticker for breaking the law.

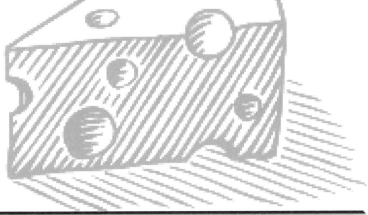

Answer:

The friend was imaginary! The strong belief of the driver that his "passenger" was real was not enough to dissuade the policeman!

5. The Doctor and the Artist

Dr. Jane Fisher was a renowned doctor. She had all sorts of patients – two of whom were world famous artists. One of the artists made Dr. Fisher very wealthy by insisting on confidentiality. How?

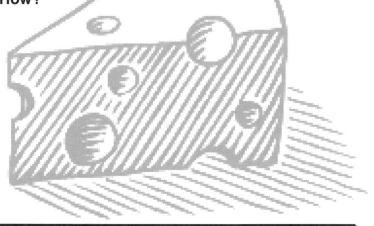

Answer:

The artist was terminally ill. He did not want anyone to know of his pending death. He advised Dr. Fisher to buy any of his available paintings before he (the patient) succumbed to his illness. All his beautiful paintings increased greatly in value upon his demise causing the paintings owned by Dr. Fisher to be worth a fortune.

6. Dominique's New Glasses

As she was being fitted for her new glasses on June 30, 2019, why could Dominique not answer the question "Where will you be one year from today?"

Answer:

She said "I don't have 20/20 vision!" (The year coming up was 2020.)

7. Paul & Adam

On Tuesday, 3/25/25, Paul and Adam, 18 year old twin brothers, were working tirelessly on solving their problem relating to getting to the college party on Friday night. They were unable to solve their problem in time to get to the party. What was their trouble?

Answer:

Someone had stolen the tires off their jointly owned car. That is why they were working "tirelessly".

8. Donna & Mark

Donna and Mark Joy's marital problems were clearly on display when their clergyman tried to help them communicate better. He asked them both the same question "What brought both of you here today?"

Donna – "Everything said he takes literally. It drives me crazy!

Mark's answer to the same question helped the clergy man see Donna's point clearly.

What was Mark's answer?

Our car! (A literal answer.)

9. Top Student

Sari made her parents very proud. She had only received straight As on her report card until the current written report. She no longer got straight A's but it made no difference to her parents of Sari. Why?

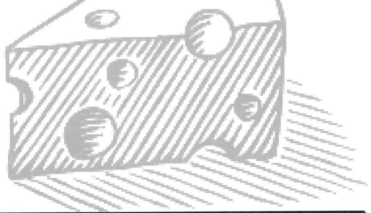

Answer:

Sari's teacher's handwriting was not neat. The A's she gave Shari were crooked – so Sari did not get "straight A's!"

10. The Initials

Bob and Al had been at summer camp for two weeks. The camp focused campers on healthy living – only allowing the eating of healthy foods. They sent a coded message to their loyal sister of four initials – not in order – knowing sister Rowena would unscramble the letters and come to their rescue. FSJP were the scrambled initials they sent.

Answer:

When unscrambled, FSJP became, PSJF – Please send junk food. She did!

11. The Family Car Trip

The family car trip was almost at an end as the family got close to their destination. A slight tapping noise coming from the engine began to worry the travelers. Mom took care of the worrying sound – without using any of the tools available in the trunk.

Answer:

Mom turned the car radio louder so no one heard the slight tapping noise above the radio voices and music.

- *11* -

12. Air Conditioner Theft

Two thieves returned the new air conditioner to the church where they had taken it – even after the church leaders publicly announced that the thieves could keep the air conditioner due to the severe heat. The wording of the "forgiveness" frightened the thieves so much they felt they had to bring it back. What was the wording?

Answer:

"Please keep the air conditioner you stole from our church because it will be very hot where you are going."

13. The Play

The musical involved some great dancing by a group of actors that had been friends and performers for years. By the end of her second week, Java was still a part of the cast, but she was no longer included in the show. Why?

Answer:

The "cast" she was part of was on her leg and her broken leg made performing impossible.

14. Horatio the TV Star

Horatio the TV Star was consistently on television. Night after night Horatio was watched by his fans on their television set, appearing on whatever channel they watched.

Answer:

Horatio was the family cat who often slept on top of the family TV while the family watched their favor it shows each night.

15. Harriet the Hen

Harriet the Hen was a miracle chicken. She did two unique things. Harriet laid square eggs! She also amazingly could actually speak a word clearly in the English language. What was the word Harriet could actually speak regularly?

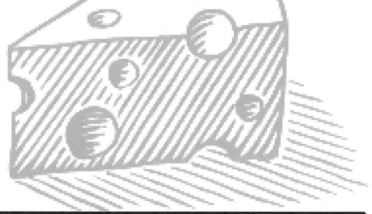

Ouch!

16. Catherine the Ballerina

On February 2020, Catherine the Ballerina bet her friend Solene that she would be able to stand on the tips of her ballet shoes for one hour by the end of June. Solene took the bet saying "I would love to see a beginning ballerina do what you just bragged you could do!" Catherine ultimately won the bet … easily. How?

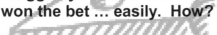

nswer:

Catherine waited until March 13, 2021. She got on her toes at 11:59 and fifty-eight seconds. Three seconds later an "hour" had passed because the clocks were turned ahead! It was then March 14, 2021.

17. Maury Counting

On Maury's first day in kindergarten, he showed his teacher, Ms. Johnson, he could count to ten by placing his fingers on his desk and counting them. He showed the teacher, Ms. Johnson, that he could indeed count higher – even though he did not know any numbers beyond 10. How did Maury do that?

Answer:

Maury raised his hands from the desk above his head and counted to 10 again. Therefore, he counted higher!

18. The Fence

Dan and Tom owned neighboring farms in Minnesota separated by a small pond. They had been best friend for years. Recently they had a serious disagreement that was so severe Dan decided to hire his trusted friend Paul to build a large fence to separate the properties. The day after Paul finished this building project, Dan and Tom became best friends again.

Answer:

Paul built a large bridge over the pond instead of a fence – which caused both men to realize that the serious disagreement" was not as important as their long friendship.

19. Albert's Trip

Albert made the last left turn by turning right to his final destination. How was that possible?

Answer:

Albert's last "left" turn was the only turn remaining in his trip. Therefore, his last turn remaining (left) was to the right. (Left means both "remaining" and "departed" - called a contronym, a word that is its own antonym.)

20. The Space Ship

The vastly advanced spaceship from a far distant galaxy was on its way to destroy Earth. For years, the benevolent world had tried to warn our planet that our divisions (country vs country, religion vs religion, depletion of food/water, global warming) were destroying any hope for the future of civilization. A last ditch brilliant idea by Mrs. Neach (a non-scientist) forced the invaders to reconsider their decision and not destroy Earth when the idea of Mrs. Neach was followed. What was Mrs. Neach's idea and what did the President of the United States order to be done?

Answer:

Pictures of smiling Earth children of all races and ages were beamed to the aliens. When the aliens saw the real future that they were going to destroy (having children of their own), they decided to give Earth another chance in the hope that the children could create a brighter future for the planet.

ABOUT THE AUTHOR

Nathan Levy

Nathan Levy is the author of more than 60 books which have sold almost 500,000 copies to teachers and parents in the US, Europe, Asia, South America, Australia and Africa. His unique <u>Stories with Holes</u> series continues to be proclaimed the most popular activity used in gifted, special education and regular classrooms by hundreds of educators. An extremely popular, dynamic speaker on thinking, writing and differentiation, Nathan is in high demand as a workshop leader in school and business settings. As a former school principal, company president, parent of four daughters and management trainer, Nathan's ability to transfer knowledge and strategies to audiences through humorous, thought provoking stories assures that participants leave with a plethora of new ways to approach their future endeavors.

Nathan Levy Books, LLC is pleased to be the publisher of this book. Teachers, students and other readers are invited to contribute their own "Stories with Holes" for possible inclusion in future volumes. Suggested stories will not be returned to you and will be acknowledged only if selected. Please send your suggestions to:

Nathan Levy Books, LLC
18 Moorland Boulevard
Monroe Township, NJ 08831
Nlevy103@comcast.net
www.storieswithholes.com

Dynamic Speakers
Creative Workshops
Relevant Topics

Nathan Levy, author of the Stories with Holes series and There Are Those, and other nationally known authors and speakers, can help your school or organization achieve positive results with children. We can work with you to provide a complete in-service package or have one of our presenters lead one of several informative and entertaining workshops.

Workshop Topics Include:

- Differentiating in the Regular Classroom
- How to Help Children Read, Write and Think Better
- Powerful Strategies to Enhance the Learning of Gifted Students
- Powerful Strategies to Help Hard to Reach Students Become More Successful Learners
- Teachers' Guide to Trauma
- Arts and Resiliency
- Gifted and Trauma
- Brain Whys – How the Brain Works
- Adoption Competent Education
- IEP/504 Facilitation

and many more...

Please write or call to receive our current catalog.
Nathan Levy Books, LLC
(732) 605-1643
NLevy103@comcast.net
www.storieswithholes.com